Super Twins
welcome
A BABY

by NATALIE BRENNER

Illustrated by
MARIE LAURE

For my 3 super sons:

There will never be adequate words to describe the depths of worth you carry. Your stories are uniquely yours, what a beautiful gift to all be interwoven together. I love you to the ends of the earth and back again, times infinity.

To our readers:

Thank you for picking this book up. We want this book to create space for uniquely-made families; there is room for all the feelings that bubble up. Let's also show our kids in traditionally-conventional families that not all families look the same. Much love!

Text Copyright © 2021 Natalie Brenner
Illustration Copyright © 2021 Marie Laure
All rights reserved, including the right and reproduction in whole or in part in any form.

ISBN: 978-0-9991634-3-6
Library of Congress
Cataloging-in-Publication Data Available

Published By
BB Books
Natalie Brenner
POB 3071
Gresham, OR
97030

www.nataliekristeen.com

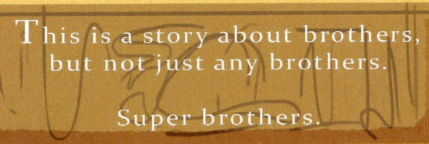

This is a story about brothers, but not just any brothers.

Super brothers.

In fact, Super Sage and Super Ira are super twins, and it's a super exciting time because there is a baby in mama's belly.

The super twins are about to become super big brothers!

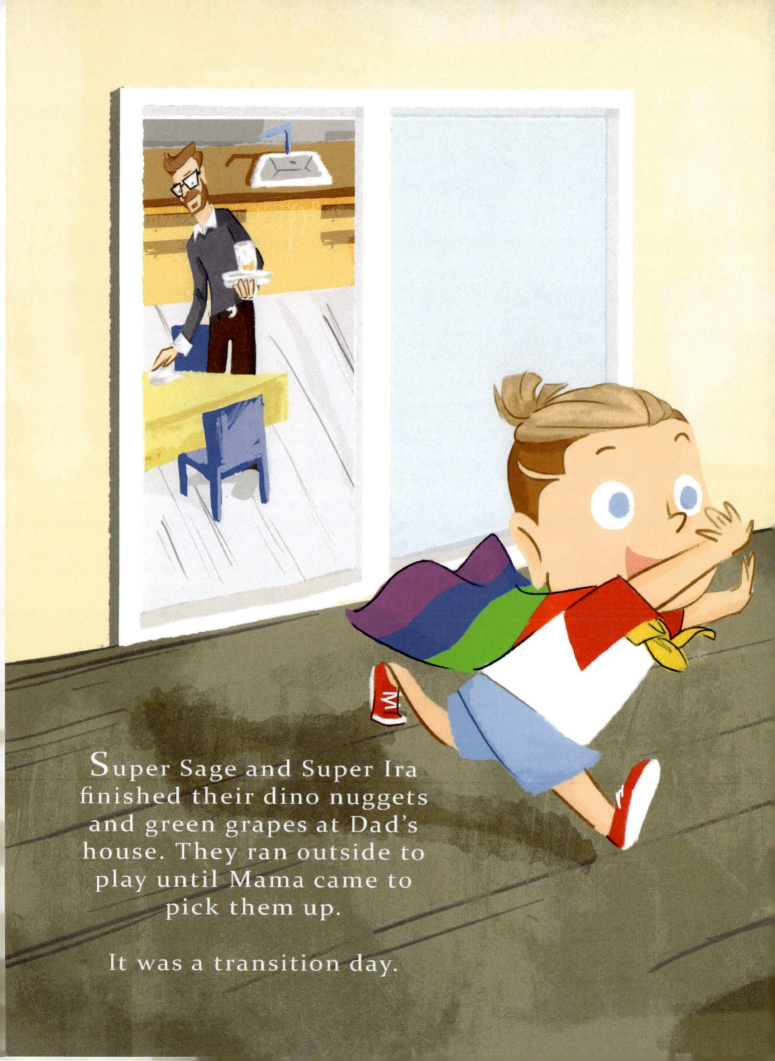

Super Sage and Super Ira finished their dino nuggets and green grapes at Dad's house. They ran outside to play until Mama came to pick them up.

It was a transition day.

While Dad cleaned the lunch mess, they zoomed through the yard wearing their rainbow capes.

Wielding sticks as swords, the super twins ran around the swing set pretending to fight off bad guys.

"Super Sage! Super Ira!"
Dad shouted from the window.
"Mama is here to pick you up.
It's time to say goodbye and see you soon.
I sure love you."

Dad met the Super Twins at the door. "Super Ira, don't forget to put on socks. Super Sage, here's your backpack with your inhaler and your dinosaur."

Mama waited at her car.

Her belly stuck out **suuuuper** far to make room for the baby inside! She smiled when she saw her Super Twins walk through Dad's door.

"Hi boys!" she said, waving super fast. "Are you ready to help get our house ready for Baby Brother?"

Super Sage and Super Ira sprinted to Mama's car.

She made sure their seat belts are on just right before climbing into her seat.
Mama looked in the mirror at them and smiled, "I sure missed you guys! But I'm glad you had fun at Dad's house."

"Are we sleeping at your house two nights?" Ira asked, holding up two fingers.

"Yes, that is the plan!" Mama said.
"Two nights at Mama's. Two nights at Dad's.
But remember,
Baby Brother can come out any
day now.
If that happens, you will go
to Dad's sooner."

Super Ira nodded.

"I didn't grow in your belly, Mama," Super Sage said.

His voice was sad as he looked out the window.

"No you didn't, Super Sage. But I love you just the same. You get to feel happy, sad, mad, or confused about being adopted. Do you want to talk about your birth mom or your adoption?" Mama asked.

"Not right now." Super Sage said.

The idea of a new baby was exciting and also kind of scary. Baby is their brother, but he would never go with them to Dad's house.

Baby had a different dad. Baby even had two more big brothers!

Sometimes, it gets a little mixed up in their heads.

Sometimes Super Sage and Super Ira are not quite sure if it is super good or super sad.

Sometimes it feels like it's both.

"Mama, will Baby want to play with us?" Super Ira asked.

"When he first comes, he will be a snuggly little person who sleeps a lot! He will eventually start to crawl and then walk and run to keep up with you two! He will want to play when he's a little older," Mama said.

"But where will Baby go when we go to Dad's house? Will he stay with you?" Super Sage asked.

"Yes! And when you come back, we'll all shout hooray! We will probably have a lot of dance parties."

She parked her big yellow car in the driveway. Mama climbed out of the car first to help unbuckle their seat belts. She moved slower because her belly was so heavy.

It was a hot summer day. Mama grabbed two mint chocolate chip ice cream cones. They sat on the patio to talk about Baby.

"What will Baby eat that's sweet?" Super Sage asked.

Mama reminded them she planned to breastfeed. It will be awhile before Baby Brother ate a sweet treat.

Super Ira asked, "Where will Baby sleep?"

Mama said, "He will be tucked up close, right next to me."

The Super Twins were super close in age:

only five months apart!

They had been together since the beginning.

They have had other brothers and sisters too.
Foster care, adoption, blended, church, and community.
There are lots of ways a family can be made. One of the super things about these Super Twins is they know families are built in a variety of unconventional ways.

Super Sage and Super Ira wanted to help get ready for Baby. They looked through their toys and picked out something special to save for Baby.

They helped Mama organize Baby's clothes.

Super Sage was excited that Baby's brown skin and curly hair would match his! Super Ira asked if Baby will come with them to preschool.

"Of course not, son. Mama's heart grows to fit more love inside! When Baby first comes, Mama might seem mad or sad. But I am not mad at or sad about you two. Having a Baby is a lot of work, but soon enough, we will find that our pieces fit together perfectly." Mama assured them, squeezed them tight, and kissed their heads goodnight.

Right as they drifted off to sleep, they were awakened.

"Super Sage! Super Ira! The plan is changing! Baby is coming. Dad is on his way to pick you up, so Baby can come out!"

Baby Brother's Daddy loaded up Mama's car. Everyone was so excited to meet Baby! Mama and Baby Brother's Daddy left to go to the hospital.

A few days later, Dad brought the Super Twins back to Mama's house to meet Baby Brother. Dad asked them if they were excited, and they said, "Maybe."

The Super Twins slowly walked into Mama's house, nervous and maybe a little scared.

She sat on the couch holding the smallest person they have ever seen, all wrapped up in a blanket. Mama had a feeling they might be nervous. She was nervous, too! More than anything, she wanted her Super Twins to know she loves them through and through.

Super Sage and Super Ira were super quiet while they looked at Baby Brother.

Mama handed them a gift from Baby. Brand new big brother capes, big brother water bottles, and superhero masks.

They stood up to give Baby Brother and Mama a hug.

"Do we get to stay here tonight?" Super Ira asked quietly.

"You boys will sleep at Dad's for a few more days while Mama's body heals. Having a baby is really owie." Mama said slowly. "I know this is hard, but soon enough we will be back to normal. It's okay to be sad. I miss you super much!"

Baby Brother is a big transition for everyone. It is super hard even if it is super good. Mama and Dad both remind the Super Twins it's okay to feel sad and happy.

One night as Mama was reading the Super Twins a bedtime story, Super Sage asked, "Are we really brothers?" Mama knew he wasn't just talking about the new baby.

"Our family might look a little unconventional. You super brothers have different dads, different stories, and different last names. What I can promise you is that this family was built with love. We love our super brothers just the same.

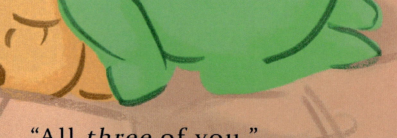

"All *three* of you."

Acknowledgements + Contributors

I express tremendous and sincerest gratitude to my sons for having inspired this book; Jasmine for always being there and helping perfect the manuscript; the incredible Alnita Coulter; the professional Ashley Ormon; proof reader and friend Stephanie Storlie; and of course to every single contributor listed + not listed without whom this book would have never been.

Special thanks to our illustrator *Marie Laure*, who has been the best illustrator I could have worked with.

Financial Contributors

Emma Le
Wing family
Cinthia Peralta
Ken and Kandy
Melissa Smith
Katie Bruckmann
Amanda K
Marcus, Lillian, & Camden
Nathalie L.S.
Wiggin's Family
Hannah Cooper
Aldén David Dwayne Alberti
Ana Nuñez
Kidd Family
Rebecca Reece
April Chapman
Kealy Family
Seth, Kara, Marlie and Baby Rogers
Tate, Archer, & Briar
Cam & Bella Kinsey
Hannah & Archer Jones
My Mom, Karen Cota
Katey Whiteman
Violet & Maisie
Kersten Family

arianiss
Deanie Whittemore
Jennifer Scarangella
Keri Bennett
Christy Bonfig
Alex & Cyrus Khosroabadi
Arianiss
Zenia BlackEagle Richert
The Henckel Family
Ashley R
Johannah Hafner
Miss Awbrie
Rich Family
Connor and Colin Wilson
Stephanie Rund
Johns Family
Jillana
Macey, Rose, & Emmy
The Maxwells
Megan Wyatt
arianiss
The VanBemmel family
Calloway Ira Blue Jacobs

Tate, Archer, & Briar
Susan Farwell
Pauline Pearce
The White Family
Yanilsa
Alyrie Thomas
Kelsey Bradley
Alyssa Fenty
Mila and Kyler
Chantelle McMullin
Katy Nicole
Vanier Family
Skylar Lamke
Shari Rahamim
Dominic & Maverick
Jaxon, Arlington, & Theodore McColly
Trisha Bledsoe
Simon, Veda and Ivy Peschong
Anne Julian
Tabitha, Frankie & Leo McHale

Made in the USA
Coppell, TX
08 August 2021